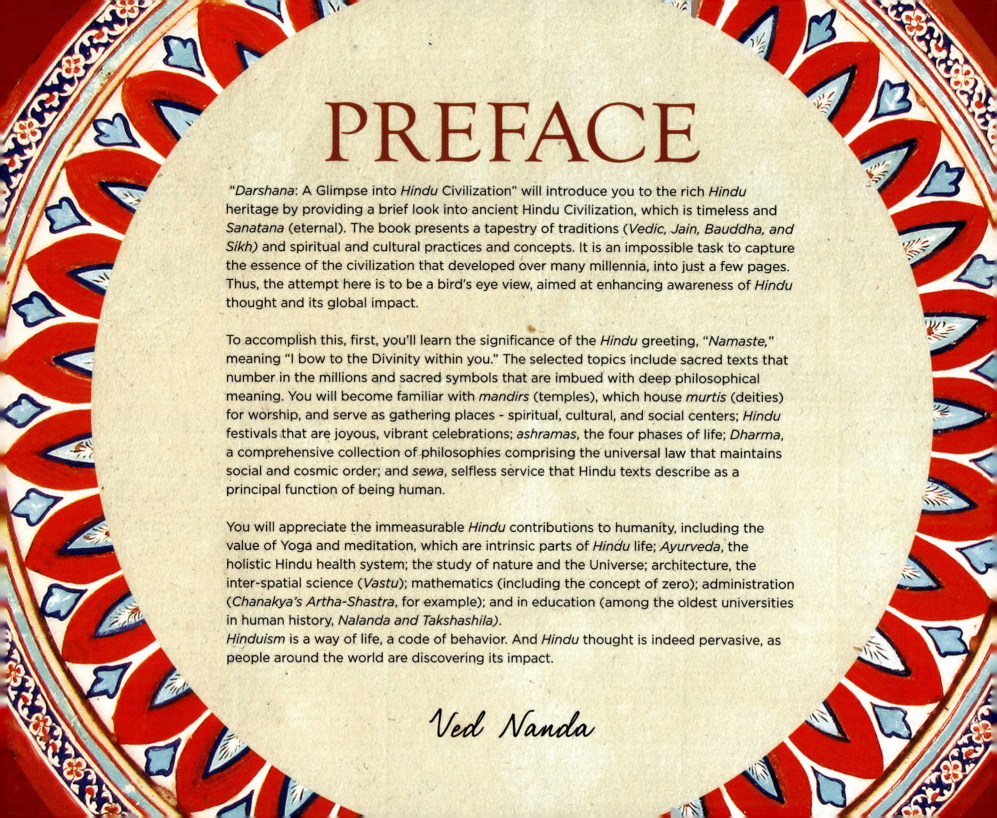

PREFACE

"*Darshana*: A Glimpse into *Hindu* Civilization" will introduce you to the rich *Hindu* heritage by providing a brief look into ancient Hindu Civilization, which is timeless and *Sanatana* (eternal). The book presents a tapestry of traditions (*Vedic, Jain, Bauddha, and Sikh)* and spiritual and cultural practices and concepts. It is an impossible task to capture the essence of the civilization that developed over many millennia, into just a few pages. Thus, the attempt here is to be a bird's eye view, aimed at enhancing awareness of *Hindu* thought and its global impact.

To accomplish this, first, you'll learn the significance of the *Hindu* greeting, "*Namaste,*" meaning "I bow to the Divinity within you." The selected topics include sacred texts that number in the millions and sacred symbols that are imbued with deep philosophical meaning. You will become familiar with *mandirs* (temples), which house *murtis* (deities) for worship, and serve as gathering places - spiritual, cultural, and social centers; *Hindu* festivals that are joyous, vibrant celebrations; *ashramas*, the four phases of life; *Dharma*, a comprehensive collection of philosophies comprising the universal law that maintains social and cosmic order; and *sewa*, selfless service that Hindu texts describe as a principal function of being human.

You will appreciate the immeasurable *Hindu* contributions to humanity, including the value of Yoga and meditation, which are intrinsic parts of *Hindu* life; *Ayurveda*, the holistic Hindu health system; the study of nature and the Universe; architecture, the inter-spatial science (*Vastu*); mathematics (including the concept of zero); administration (*Chanakya's Artha-Shastra*, for example); and in education (among the oldest universities in human history, *Nalanda and Takshashila*).
Hinduism is a way of life, a code of behavior. And *Hindu* thought is indeed pervasive, as people around the world are discovering its impact.

Ved Nanda

Ved Nanda

Distinguished University Professor, University of Denver
Director, Ved Nanda Center for International Law,
University of Denver Sturm College of Law
Honorary Professor, University of Delhi Faculty of Law (India)

FOREWORD

Hinduism is the veritable Sanatana Dharma, the eternal and ever renewed manifestation of the universal pursuit of truth, the Divine and Self-realization, at a practical and at a transcendent level.

Hinduism is the oldest, most diverse and perhaps most profound religion and spiritual teaching in history, with an influence on all humanity, not only outwardly through its teachings but inwardly through the spiritual force of its great *rishis, yogis, gurus*, sages and seers, which today have millions of followers on every continent. As such Hinduism is relevant to everyone and essential for understanding our place and purpose as a species and our inner capacity for a higher consciousness.

Yet because of its vastness and the fact that it cannot be reduced to any formula, creed or doctrine, *Hinduism* is also the most misunderstood and misrepresented of the world's religions, though it is the third largest religion in the world, and the largest and most enduring of the non-Abrahamic and indigenous traditions. Because of this a new look at *Hinduism* is essential.

A new, simple and clear presentation of *Sanatana Dharma* is essential for understanding the deeper spiritual and cultural heritage of humanity. The *Darshana* Coffee Table Book fills this purpose. It is an excellent presentation of *Hinduism* that can communicate and appeal to every person, social and age group, about this wonderful tradition. Most importantly it is a presentation from the *Hindu* community itself and its important teachers and organizations, so its views are from inside of Hinduism by those who practice it, not simply from the outside by those who may not understand its many levels and dimensions.

The *Darshana* Coffee Table Book contains an excellent set of posters, illustrations and descriptions of *Hindu dharma*. It provides the reader a succinct key to every aspect of life, knowledge and culture from a *Hindu* perspective. It can be used as a primer on Hinduism for schools, organizations and individuals. It is particularly relevant today when Hindus have spread worldwide through a great diaspore and Hindu temples can be found in cities and communities East and West. I will summarize a few of these key points below.

Hinduism is first of all a science, *vidya or Veda*, a way of cosmic and Self-knowledge as integrally related. It shows how the entire universe is mirrored within each one of us, all creatures and every aspect of the world. This *Hindu* way of knowledge encompasses both spiritual and practical sciences. It includes medicine, psychology, cosmology, linguistics, mathematics and much more.

Yet *Hinduism* is an art, encompassing all aspects of culture, music, dance, sculpture, painting and architecture. As a sacred art it encompasses the largest set of temples and sacred sites in the world. *Hinduism* has the world's largest set of festivals and celebrations in which all these myriad aspects of culture and spirituality are shared.

Hinduism is not simply a matter of belief or concepts, it is a way of life. Yet it is a way of living in harmony with the whole of life, regarding all life as sacred, and each individual being as connected to the whole of life. *Hinduism* is also an ecology that teaches us our proper harmonious interrelationship with every aspect of existence, animate and inanimate, seeing the Divine everywhere.

Perhaps most importantly *Hinduism* is a way of Self-realization, teaching each individual how to discover and manifest their true Self, *Atman or Purusha,* which is the ultimate goal for all of us.

Hinduism encompasses all the ways of worshipping and approaching the Divine through every type of path and every aspect of the human being, whether knowledge *(jnana)*, devotion *(bhakti)*, action *(karma)* interwoven into the many paths of Yoga from *Hatha to Raja* and the many different systems of Hindu philosophy through *Vedanta and Tantra.* These teachings are set forth by ancient and modern gurus in every generation to be relevant to each person, time, place and culture.

Darshana is a book of vision and a book to live with. It opens us up to the inner vision of *Sanatana Dharma.* Try understanding one of its topics every day or every week, carefully considering its teachings and their applications in our own lives.

We thank the team that has put together this wonderful presentation of *Hindu Dharma* over many years, and refined it to the essence. It is a book that is both easy to access and yet relevant to all the main issues of life, summarizing the Hindu vision for all. We hope that its teachings are widely shared to race humanity in our current time of crisis.

Vamadeva Shastri

Vamadeva Shastri (David Frawley)
American Hindu teacher and author

CONTENTS

NAMASTE

Recognition of Divinity

Namaste is commonly used as both a greeting and a parting phrase. It means:
"I bow to the divinity within you."

नमस्ते

NAMASTE   **NUH-MUHS-THAY**

The *Hindu* civilization - or the *Dharmic* civilization - is one of the most ancient in the world.

The various traditions which were born from the Indian subcontinental region are united by *Dharmic* principles and are incredibly diverse in philosophy, culture, language, and practice.

This *Dharmic* diversity supported the development of numerous sophisticated disciplines which continue to contribute to key fields of human endeavor. These include various evolving philosophies, sciences, arts, architecture, and more. This exhibition offers a bird's eye view of *Hindu* philosophies and practices.

Bhagavad Gita, Chapter 9, Verse 29

"समो ऽहं सर्वभूतेषु"
i reside in all beings

Rig Veda, 1.89.1

"आनो भद्राः क्रतवो यन्तु विश्वतः"
Let noble thoughts come from everywhere

Rig Veda, 1.164.46

"एकं सद्विप्रा बहुधा वदन्ति "
Truth is one, the wise say it in many ways

Bhagavad Gita, Chapter 5, Verse 18

"पण्डिताः समदर्शिनः"
The wise look at everything with equanimity

MANDIR

Spiritual and Cultural Centers

Mandirs are considered to be potent locations of invoked divinity. A *mandir* houses a *murti* or several *murtis*, which are physical figures and embodiments of divine qualities.

The presence of these *murtis* and the associated rituals are understood to cultivate a distinct atmosphere which is conducive to human development and spiritual elevation. For this reason, mandirs have been the center of spiritual, social, and intellectual life throughout the *Hindu* region, serving as a nucleus around which artistic and cultural activities can flourish.

Of note, *mandirs* are well-renowned for their intricate and sometimes structurally baffling architecture.

SYMBOLS

Profound Meaning, Condensed

Hindu symbols, which are representative of core *Dharmic* principles, can be commonly found on everyday objects, around households, in rituals, and in Divine imagery. They are both remembrances of sacred *Dharmic* concepts and reminders to reflect upon them.

AUM

This vibration, or sound, is believed to be the sound with which existence came into being and which continues to resound everywhere at all times. By generating the resonance of *aum,* we are able to tune into the Divine.

SHANKHA

A *shankha* is a conch shell, often seen in the hands of *Hindu* deities, which represents transformation. Conch shells are blown to mark an auspicious beginning.

RANGOLI / KOLAM

Rangolis are sacred geometric patterns drawn in front of doorways or entrances to invoke auspiciousness and welcome prosperity.

The vibration created by properly uttering *Aum* is said to resonate with the underlying vibrations running through the universe.

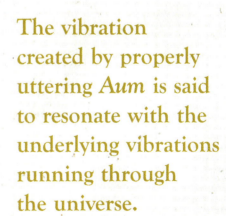

BINDI / TILAK

The *bindi* or *tilak* marks the location of the *ajna chakra* within the brain. It is traditionally made from an herbal substance and is symbolic of a person's spiritual orientation.

YOGA

Fundamental Theory

Yoga is derived from the *Samskrit* root *'yuj'* meaning *'to yoke'* or to be in union. Thus, yoga is 'the yoking of' or the realization of Unity between the individual self and Divine Self. This process of yoga is several thousands of years old and is still widely practiced.

Of the various methods dedicated to the process of yoga, Sage *Patanjali's* Yoga *Sutras* are said to have outlined its essential philosophy most succinctly. In the *sutras, Patanjali* describes yoga as being "eight-limbed", the limbs of which are as follows:

The *asana* limb of yoga is commonly misconceived as being the entirety of the process.

While practicing the *asana* limb of yoga brings many health benefits, these benefits are relatively incomplete and early milestones within a more holistic process of gaining clarity and stability, and becoming capable of achieving *samadhi.*

1. YAMA
Taking up principles which are unwavering

2. NIYAMA
Taking up practices which are unceasing

8. SAMADHI
Being blissfully absorbed in contemplation

3. ASANA
Bringing harmony to body and mind through mindful physical postures

7. DHYANA
Maintaining uninterrupted concentration on a subject of contemplation

4. PRANAYAMA
Regulating body energy cycles through controlled breathing

6. DHARANA
Focusing attention on a subject of contemplation

5. PRATYAHARA
Overcoming indulgence through restraint over one's senses

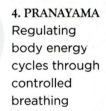

DIVINITY

Diversity and Representation

Hindu Dharma is a comprehensive collection of philosophies in which the concept of Divinity ranges from a **negation** of the existence of the Divine, to **agnosticism**, to **firm conviction** in the existence of a single, all pervasive, independent, immanent and transcendent Divinity called *"brahman"*.

Vedic philosophy identifies co-existing feminine and masculine aspects of Divinity.

DIVINITY AS FEMININE

The Feminine aspect is recognized, revered, and worshipped as *shaktih* and in the forms of *Durga, Lakshmi, Saraswati,* etc. who each represent qualities and essences which exist in Nature and can be invoked.

DIVINE IMAGERY

Because the *Hindu Dharmic* system is a pluralistic one, there are no mandates regarding the representation of the Divine. The Divine is recognized in the form of a child, a plant, a many-armed metaphorical deity, or equally, as formless and quality-less.

DIVINITY IN NATURE

Hindus regard everything around them and throughout existence to be pervaded by Divinity. So, local mountains, rivers, cows, the *tulsi* plant, etc. are revered, making sustainable and eco-friendly practice integral to *Dharma*.

DHARMA

The Intrinsic Order of Existence

Dharma is the natural, eternal, and universal law that maintains cosmic and social order. Humans' *dharma* comprises the duties of an individual towards family, society, humanity, and the environment. **Dharma is the natural order underlying existence.** The eternal principles of *dharma* form the basis of the philosophies, beliefs, and practices that originated in the Indian sub-continent such as *Hindu Dharma, Bauddha Dharma, Jain Dharma, and Sikh Dharma.*

Dharma is an all-encompassing term that **links truth and human activity** in accordance with the natural laws that govern the cosmos. Traditions such as *Bauddha Dharma* highlight this link.

Dharma for individuals consists of some **general principles** such as forgiveness and patience, which allow for clear decision-making and **righteous behavior.**

Dharma is **unique** in every situation. The various scriptures complement one's lived experience and conscience, and offer guidance on how to **determine one's own *dharma.***

Dharma is both why things are as they are and the path to understanding it.

In some traditions, such as the *Jain* tradition, *dharma* is the **conduct of a human being** within their role as a house-holder or an ascetic.

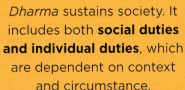

Dharma is the **common thread** which binds the **various philosophies** born from the Indian subcontinent.

Dharma sustains society. It includes both **social duties and individual duties**, which are dependent on context and circumstance.

SPIRITUAL PATHS

The Four Yogas

The process of realizing Unity between the individual self and the Divine self can happen through different paths or orientations. All of the possible lifestyles which are conducive to yoga have been distilled into four essential spiritual paths:

These spiritual paths are referenced in the *Bhagvad Gita*

the most widely-revered *Hindu* text - and are able to accommodate the various **inclinations** of people, their **natures**, and the changes they experience through the **phases** of their life.

JNANA YOGA

the path of engaging rigorously with knowledge, wisdom, and philosophy

KARMA YOGA

the path of selfless and detached work dedicated to universal well-being

BHAKTI YOGA

the path of devotion, in which selfless Love for the Divine drives all thought and behavior

RAJA YOGA

the path of exercising self-control over one's psyche to master one's passions and motivations

TRADITIONS

Vedic, Jain, Bauddha, and Sikh

Many spiritual traditions arose out of the *Dharmic* foundation of the Indian subcontinent, the most general and popular of which are the *Vedic, Bauddha, Jain* and *Sikh* traditions. While they share some common principles, there is great diversity between these traditions and variation within each one as well.

BAUDDHA DHARMA

is based upon the teachings of *Buddha* and contains the principles, among others, of *dharma, karma, ahimsa* and rebirth. *Bauddha Dharma* is guided by the *Tripitaka* scriptures and consists of practices such as meditation, the chanting of hymns, and *sangha*, or collective living.

Those who live according to this tradition of *Dharma* strive for nirvana, marking the cessation of desire and eradication of all suffering.

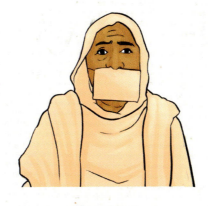

SIKH DHARMA

is a way of life developed upon the spiritual teachings of *Guru Nanak. Sikhs' Guru Granth Sahib* articulates systems of niau, or moral justice, remembrance of Divine *naam,* or Divine name, and union with *akaal*, or Timeless Divinity.

VEDIC DHARMA

the oldest *Dharmic* tradition, is colloquially referred to as *Hindu Dharma* or traditionally as *Sanatana Dharma.* It is based upon the knowledge of the Vedas and contains the principles of *dharma* and *karma,* which incorporate concepts like *ahimsa* and rebirth. Those who live according to this *Dharmic* tradition strive for *moksha,* which is the experience of sat-chit-ananda or realizing Unity with the Divine.

The ways in which *Hindus* progress towards *moksha* are various, keeping with the belief that "the wise pursue Truth in numerous ways and know the Divine by many names" as proclaimed in the *Rig Veda.*

JAIN DHARMA

follows the teachings of *Mahavir.* This tradition emphasizes the principle of *ahimsa*, non-violence, not only towards living things, but towards all existence. This informs *Jains'* dietary practices and other core principles such as non-absolutism and non-possessiveness. This tradition also contains the concepts of rebirth and *moksha.*

SACRED TEXTS

Origin and Transfer of Knowledge

The Indian National Mission for Manuscripts, in 2013, listed 3.5 million *Hindu* manuscripts out of the estimated 40 million in India. Over 60% of these have yet to be translated for the first time.

While *Hindu* knowledge transfer took place orally over centuries, a lot of it was also well-recorded in text and maintained in *mandirs* and university libraries, offering wide-ranging knowledge through poetry and prose.

THE 4 VEDAS

- Rig Veda
- Sama Veda
- Yajur-Veda
- Atharva Veda

DARSHANA SHASTRAS

- Nyaya-Vaisheshika
- Sankhya-Yoga
- Mimamsa & Vedanta - Advaitha
- Vishishtadvaita and Dvaita

UPANISHADS & BRAHMA-SUTRAS

The two most commented upon bodies of the *shruti* texts.

BHAGAVAD GITA

A portion of *Mahabharata*, made up of 700 slokas. It is the most published, widely read and recited philosophical and theistic treatise on the core concepts of *Hindu Dharma*.

SMRITI TEXTS

Often suggest a code of conduct, as in the *Parashara smriti* and *Manu smriti*.

JAIN AND BUDDHIST TEXTS

The *Jain Agamas* and *Buddhist Tripitakas* are fundamental texts for the *Jain* and *Buddhist Dharmic* traditions.

ITIHASAS AND PURANAS

These histories include the *Mahabharata, Ramayana, and Bhagavata Purana,* which illustrate the knowledge of the *Vedas* through narrative.

AGAMA TEXTS

Instructional theistic texts explaining modes and methods of the worship of deities in temples.

GURU GRANTH SAHIB

Teachings of *Sikh Dharma* flow down through *Guru Granth Sahib.*

ASHRAMAS

The four phases of life

Through the four phases of life, a person's sense of
identity expands from their individual self, to their
family, to their community, and eventually, to the Divine.

SANYASA
The renouncement phase of life is devoted fully to spirituality.

BRAHMACHARYA
The student phase of life is meant to be simple and focused completely on education.

VANAPRASTHA
The retired phase of life is when time is devoted to social service, pilgrimage, and spiritual reflection.

Through the allocation of priorities, people can maximize their spiritual development as well as generate societal prosperity.

GRIHASTHA
The householder phase of life is when attention is given to providing for the family and raising children.

PURSUITS

Four Human Motivations

In *Hindu* philosophy, human pursuits are broken up into four categories. A person can lead a balanced and fulfilling life by following each of these pursuits simultaneously. The pursuit of any one of the four categories should not violate the pursuit of any of the others.

DHARMA

The pursuit of harmonious living, virtuous conduct, and social order through the fulfillment of duties, rights, and laws.

KAMA

The pursuit of aesthetic enjoyment, passions, affection, love, and the fulfillment of wishes and emotions.

ARTHA

The pursuit of the material means which enable a person to live as they please, involving financial and economic prosperity.

MOKSHA

The pursuit of liberation from the entanglements of life and rebirth, and of realizing unity with the Divine.

This balance between ethics, passions, materialism, and spirituality

allows a person to fulfill the natural human motivations without overindulging in any one of them or creating depravity or disorder.

SEWA

Divine Service

Sewa, or selfless service, has been described in various sacred *Hindu* texts as a paramount function of being human. Universal well-being is achieved through the selfless service of all things, all beings, and all people.

ENVIRONMENT

Every human life is brought about and maintained by a number of factors: ancestors, Divinity, society, plants, insects, etc. So, every human owes it to each of these factors to look after their well-being, and to do so without any selfish or expectation-oriented intention.

Sewa is done out of a selfless, Divine love.

DIVINITY

Because Divinity is all-pervading, selfless service toward anyone or anything is considered Divine service. Moreover, it is every person's dharma to do *sewa* of their family members, nearby animals, plants, and their local community since selfless service, performed out of love, is the means by which natural and social order are maintained.

FESTIVALS

Celebration and Spirituality

Hindu festivals are joyous, vibrant celebrations and occasions of self-reflection. The various festivals **honor natural phenomena** such as seasonal change and harvest, **commemorate incarnations of Divinity**, and **celebrate familial and social relationships**.
Most festivals are marked by the *Hindu* lunar calendar.

The following are but a few examples of *Hindu* festivals, which are countless and vary geographically not only within the Indian subcontinent but around the world.

VIJAYA DASHAMI

Dussehra celebrates the victory of good over evil and, in particular, honors the divine Feminine. As the story goes, at a time when a disruptive force called *Mahishasura* endangered the natural Order of existence, a great feminine Energy emerged to overcome this evil.

Many other stories and instances are also honored during this festival. In particular, the importance of unity and combined strength is highlighted and reflected upon.

DEEPAVALI (DIWALI)

Commonly termed 'the festival of lights', *deepavali* extends over a five-day period and is celebrated by lighting earthen lamps (deepa) and firecrackers, among other practices, to commemorate the homecoming of *Shri Rama*, who is recognized as an incarnation of the Divine. Other events are also remembered during this festival as *Hindus* invoke abundance, prosperity, and the victory of knowledge over ignorance.

RAKSHA BANDHAN

Raksha bandhan celebrates human relationships and community. People tie a rakhi, or thread, around the wrists of the people they love and invoke their protection. Many traditional stories highlight instances where a person wearing a rakhi is protected in the face of imminent danger.

The festival cultivates a sense of collective responsibility for the protection of one another. Recently, the practice has become more commonly performed between brother and sister, but historical and contemporary instances indicate that the tying of a *rakhi* holds significance within any relationship or bond.

CALENDAR

Hindu Time Keeping

The study of the *Vedas* requires a prerequisite understanding of the *Vedangas* and of *Jyotisha*, texts which explain time-keeping through a study of the movements of the Sun, Moon, and Earth along with other astronomical phenomena.

KUMBHA
Aquarius

MINA
Pisces

MESHA
Aries

MAKARA
Capricorn

VRISHABHA
Taurus

DHANU
Sagittarius

MITHUNA
Gemini

VRISHCHIKA
Scorpio

KARKA
Cancer

TULA
Libra

SIMHA
Leo

KANYA
Virgo

These texts, and subsequent studies, calculated the number of days it took for the Earth to revolve around the Sun, and for the Moon to revolve around the Earth. They categorized these periods into lunar months and thus, precisely calculated eclipses, laid foundation to a 7-day week, and developed a system to map the zodiac constellations. The *Hindu* lunar calendar which resulted from these studies is called the *Panchanga*, or the five-limbed calendar, which has an advanced capability of predicting astrological phenomena and keeping time.

AYURVEDA

Hindu Health Sciences

Ayurveda, the *Hindu* health science as explained several thousand years ago in the *Vedas*, takes a **holistic** approach to understanding life by basing diet, medicine, treatments, and practices on an understanding of the **flow of energy** through the body.

Commonly practiced even today, *Ayurveda* goes beyond the mere treatment of symptoms and, by addressing the subtler imbalances or impediments within the body, prescribes medicines, treatments, and practices with **minimal side effects**. These are based on the understanding of the elements and their combinations within the body.

FIRE   WATER

PITTA

EARTH   WATER

KAPHA

AIR   ETHER

VAATA

Prescribes personalized diet and lifestyle based on body composition and contextual factors such as geographic and climatic conditions.

Uses natural **substances** and processes to enhance health

Not only curative, but **preventative**

KEY FIGURES

Acharya Charaka - Revered for the development of medicine
🌿 Described medicinal qualities and functions of 100,000 herbal plants.
🌿 Revealed various facts on human anatomy, embryology, pharmacology, blood circulation, and diseases like diabetes, tuberculosis, heart disease, etc.

Sushruta - Revered for great strides in surgery
🌿 Described over 300 operations and 42 surgical instruments.
🌿 His texts reached Persia and the Arab world in the 8th century and reached Europe in the 12th century, having great influence over medieval Western surgical development.

HINDU ARTS

Divine Expression

Divinity in *Vedic* philosophy is all-pervading, the representations of life, experience, and beauty are also representations of the Divine. The arts of rhythm, dance, sculpture, painting, warfare, etc. are founded with the intention of giving expression to the Divine and are detailed among 64 kalas, or art forms, in ancient scriptures.

DANCE

The *Natya Shastra*, written by *Bharata Muni* around the 4th century BCE, is the oldest surviving text on stagecraft, detailing different postures, facial expressions and mudras, or hand expressions. *Hindu* dance combines advanced techniques of story-telling with pure rhythmic movements, offering contemporary interpretations of traditional *Hindu* epics and innovating methods of expression through body movement. *Hindu* dance begins and ends with a prayer, and the entirety of dance is performed as an act of devotion.

Hindu arts are an expression of devotion.

MUSIC

Foundations of music in *Hindu* traditions can be found in the *Sama Veda* , one of the four *Vedas*, which are the fundamental collections of *Hindu* inquiry and philosophy. The *Sama Veda* is studied by modern musicians and outlines numerous melodies, rhythms, and methods of chanting, giving *Hindu* music its foundational structure.

MARTIAL ARTS

Rishi Parshuram is said to have invented *Kalaripayattu*, an ancient martial art involving a sword and shield. Today, *Kalaripayattu* is most commonly practiced in southern India, where men and women who have studied the tradition preserve and pass down the ancient method. *Mall-yuddha*, or wrestling, and *Silambam* are other forms of *Hindu* martial arts built on ancient curricula.

ROCK CARVINGS / SCULPTING

Rock carving and sculpting can be traced back to at least 3000 BCE in the Harappan civilization. Its continuity is evident across the Indian subcontinent. For example, the Ellora Caves, a UNESCO World Heritage site, feature carvings of scenes from the *Mahabharata*, a *Hindu* epic. These carvings are accredited to *Hindu, Buddhist*, and *Jain* history, and showcase not only great variety and historical progression, but harmony between arious traditions.

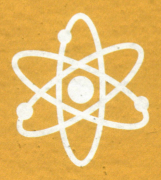

SCIENCES

Hindu Inquiry

The study of nature and the universe through the sciences of biology, metallurgy, physics, and other fields was deeply intertwined with the process of pursuing the Divine. *Vedic* texts, poetry, architecture, and rituals display a great interest and remarkable development within these sciences.

METALLURGY

Production and purification of metals and alloys goes hand in hand with technological advancement. Many experiments and best practices are found in texts dating to the 3rd and 4th centuries BCE, and in artifacts from the *Hindu Saraswati* civilization. The study of metallurgy is said to have reached its pinnacle with the creation of a metallurgical marvel called the **Vishnu Stambh**. The stambh is an ancient pillar weighing over three tons which, till date, has not begun to rust and is considered to be rust-resistant.

The antiquity of *Hindu* chemical traditions can be traced back to the *Vedas*, the most ancient and foundational Dharmic texts.

BIOLOGY

The *Hindu* study of life included botany and anatomy, leading to the development of medicine, agriculture, arbori-horticulture, and other health sciences. **The Rig Veda, Vrikshayurveda, Atharva Veda** and other texts contain classifications of plants based on descriptions of their growth behavior, physiology and sensorial behaviors, processes for nourishment, pathologies, reproductive patterns, and medicinal properties. Some biological observations are so astute that they suggest the use of a strong magnifying tool with microscopic capabilities.

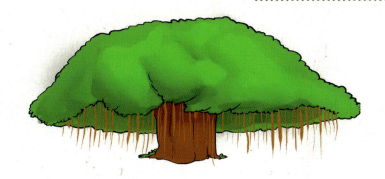

ATOMIC AND NUCLEAR PHYSICS

While discoveries in atomic physics are relatively new, *Hindu* scriptures contain many remarkably similar ideas. For example, the *Vedas* mention *paramanu* as a type of substance which cannot be split further. *Rishi Kanada* elaborates further in his *Vaisheshika Sutras* by discussing *anu*, which are indestructible and can bond to form pairs or triplets. He notes that unseen forces cause interactions between these *anu*. Clearly, these texts contain some knowledge of atoms and quarks, among other modern concepts. These similarities are recognized at CERN today, where a large *Hindu Nataraja* figure is featured.

ARCHITECTURE

Holistic Spatial Science

Hindu spatial science, or the science of *vaastu*, can be traced back to the *Vedas* and involves the disciplines of mathematics, acoustics, astrology, arts, philosophy, and a deep understanding of the environment. This holistic science finds its expression in the architecture of civic buildings and mandirs as well as in expert city planning, the construction of canals, and more.

Ancient settlements found at *Dholavira* and *Mohenjo-Daro,* among other *Indus* River Valley settlements, have sophisticated water conservation systems.

The hydraulic engineering discovered in these settlements make the oldest and most expansive sanitation systems in the world, featuring wells, reservoirs, channels, storage tanks, stone-cut troughs, and rivulets. The infrastructure dates back to earlier than 2500 BCE, and some of it has even been conserved over the ages and developed into present-day use.

CHAUSATH YOGINI MANDIR
MORENA, MADHYA PRADESH, 11TH CENTURY CE

This *mandir* has remained structurally sound for over a millennium, despite high seismic activity, due to its circular floor plan, which has greater resistance to seismic forces than box-shaped structures.

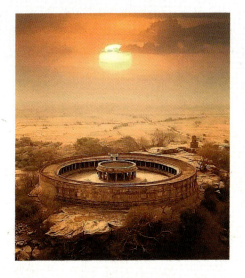

CHAND BAORI
JAIPUR, RAJASTHAN, 9TH CENTURY CE

Chand Baori is a 13-story deep step well with 3500 symmetrical steps. It was a reservoir and gathering spot for locals during festive events and it maintained a low temperature in the hot region of *Rajasthan.*

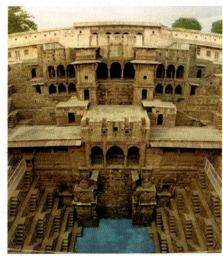

MUSICAL PILLARS
HAMPI, KARNATAKA, 7TH CENTURY CE

Solid stone pillars adorn this *temple* which, when tapped, sound like musical notes. Tapping several of these pillars creates sounds similar to the *Mridanga,* an Indian musical instrument. There are also similar temples with musical pillars in *Tirunelveli* and *Madurai, Tamil Nadu.*

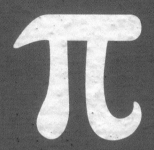

MATHEMATICS

Hindu Contributions

The *Vedic Hindu* tradition made several key mathematical discoveries, like the concept of zero and the decimal system, and developed algebra, arithmetic, and geometry. These mathematics spread across the world through translation into Arabic, Latin, and eventually contemporary Western thought.

Trignometry was a key *Hindu* contribution to the world of mathematics. The *Sanskrit "jya"* and *"koti jya"* are known as "sine" and "cosine".

Area of Triangle
Aryabhata (476 CE) explained that the area of a triangle is the product of half of any side and the perpendicular distance from that side to the opposite vertex.

Hindu philosophy, which contains the study of logic and the concept of *shunya*, formed the basis for *Hindu* mathematical inquiry, giving rise to the mathematical concept of zero and advanced usage of geometry. A modern example of *Hindu* philosophy informing mathematics is that of *S. Ramanujan* (1887-1920), whose mathematics were an expression of his devotion to the *Hindu* goddess, *Lakshmi*.

π

Madhava (1340-1425 CE) listed the **value of pi** to 11 decimal places: 3.1415926539. Later, *Karnapadhati* described the value to 17 decimal places.

Zero:
from *"shunya"* in *Sanskrit*, to "si-fr" in Arabic to "ziffre" in Latin to "zero" in Western tradition.

S. Ramanujan (1887-1920),
credited with game theory and infinite series, described math as an expression of his devotion to *Lakshmi*.

Early *Hindu Brahmi* Numerals 300 BCE - 400 CE

Madhava (1350 CE) made advances in **infinite series** including finding the expansions for trigonometric functions.

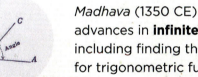

EDUCATION

Ancient Schools And Universities

Hindu universities were among the oldest in human history, drawing students seeking higher education from across the world. Of these universities, *Nalanda* and *Takshashila* were incredibly popular, offering specializations in the STEM fields, arts, and political sciences.

The transition from ignorance to knowledge is a common motif

in *Hindu* philosophy, as is reverence towards teachers. The process of gaining education and the role of teachers continue to be very highly esteemed among *Hindus*.

Hindus, for ages, have celebrated the phases of education. Toddlers would be initiated into primary schooling, and teenagers into higher studies at *gurukulas*, or residential schools.

Representative map of India before 1947

Takshashila
Nalanda
Odantapuri
Jagaddala
Somapura
Varanasi/Kashi
Vallabhi
Vikramshila
Pushpagiri
Nagarjunakonda
Kanchipuram

Following in the footsteps of ancient female scholars and sages such as *Gargi, Maitreyi, Vagambhrini, and Lopamudra,* women underwent rigorous, holistic schooling. Today, the same culture is a world leader in producing female STEM graduates.

ADMINISTRATION

Kingdoms Over the Centuries

Mahabharata's Anushasana Parva chapter and the
Artha-Shastra by *Chanakya* are two prominent works on
warfare and administration, discussing military, trade,
and governance techniques that balance people's worldly
well-being and spiritual pursuits.

WARFARE

The *Mauryan* empire, as recorded by Greek historians circa 300 BCE, boasted the world's largest army at the time, with 600,000 in infantry, 30,000 in cavalry, and 9,000 in war elephants. Guerilla warfare tactics used by the *Ahom* kings of Northeastern India and the naval expeditions of Emperor *Shivaji* also marked periods of **exemplary military development.**

The principles of administration are integral to several *Dharmic* texts.

TRADE

Persian and European travelers referred to *Vijayanagara* as the richest region in the world, where precious stones and metal were traded on the streets of its capital, *Hampi. Hindu* kingdoms **attracted traders from across the world** and contributed to half of the world's GDP by the 15th century CE.

Records also show that economic power did not always rest with monarchies, but was wielded by publicly owned **corporations** such as *Manigramam*. These were governed by a code of conduct outlined by *banaju-dharma*, which is still practiced by merchants to ensure the continuity of **ethical business.**

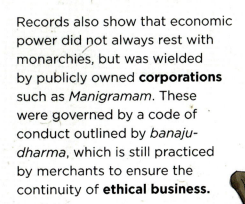

FEMALE LEADERS

During colonial times, the military prowess of *Hindu* kingdoms, and especially of **female leaders**, were noted by British authorities. Figures like Queen *Laxmibai* of *Jhansi* and Queen *Chennamma of Kittur* were among numerous excellent swordswomen and **strategists** across India who defended their kingdoms against invasion.

GLOBAL IMPACT

Hindus Around the World

Dharmic traditions and philosophies have spread across the world through trade and immigration despite never proselytizing. The pluralistic orientation of *Dharma* makes it universal, capable of coexisting with local philosophies and practices across the globe.

A statue in a *Hindu mandir* in Indonesia

Archeological excavations point to the existence of *Hindu Dharma* in the region over 2000 years ago.

HINDU DHARMA IN ASIA

The largest *Hindu temple* in the world is located in *Cambodia,* a testament to how widespread *Hindu Dharma* was in *Southeast Asia.* As shown by newer monuments in *Malaysia*, and through local art and theatre in Indonesia featuring *Hindu epics,* these are popular even today.

The remains of *Bamiyan Buddha* statues in Afghanistan and ruins of the grand Sun Temple in Pakistan's *Multan* are examples of *Dharmic* presence in the central and western regions of Asia.

A South African *Hindu* women

Diwali motorcade in Guyana

HINDU DHARMA IN SOUTH AMERICA

European colonialism brought *Hindus* to the Caribbean region and South America, where *Dharmic* philosophies and practices were passed down and also blended with indigenous and Afro-Caribbean culture. Today, over 500,000 *Hindu*s live in South America, most of whom have never visited India, and continue to practice *Sanatana Dharma.*

HINDU DHARMA IN AFRICA

Recorded history shows evidence of trade between ancient Indian and African kingdoms, which shared striking similarities in customs and traditions. *Hindus* later went to Africa during the colonial era, bringing their various spiritual traditions with them.

GLOBAL CENTERS

Mandirs Around the World

Today, *Hindu mandirs* exist across the globe, serving as spiritual, cultural, and social centers for *Hindu* communities to come together, engage in their spiritual practices, and preserve their culture.

PASHUPATINATH TEMPLE, NEPAL

Dedicated to *Shiva*, this mandir dates back to 400 BCE. It is located within the *Kathmandu* valley in *Nepal.*

ANGKOR WAT TEMPLE, CAMBODIA

The most visited tourist attraction in Cambodia and the world's largest *Hindu mandir,* this *mandir* was built in the 12th century and is spread over 400 acres of land.

SRI KAALI AMMAN TEMPLE, MYANMAR

Built by *Tamil* migrants in 1871, the *Shri Kali Mandir of Yangon, Myanmar* is a major focal point of the city's unofficial "Little India".

SRI SIVA SUBRAMANIYA SWAMI TEMPLE, FIJI

Located in Nadi, Fiji, at the very end of the main road through the city, the *Shri Shiva Subramaniya Swami Mandir* is the largest mandir in the whole Pacific region.

SRI KRISHNA MANDIR, OMAN

Built by the *Gujarati* community of *Muscat, Oman,* this beautiful *mandir* is a popular place of worship and celebration, especially during the festival of *Navratri.*

ARYA DEWAKER MANDIR, SURINAME

Built by the Arya Dewakar *Hindu* group, this mandir is the most prominent in Suriname and is visited by both *Hindus* and non-*Hindu*s alike.

FUN FACTS

Statistical data on dharma

The following are some assorted numerical estimates
regarding Dharmic cultures and their global presence.

1 in 4 people worldwide follow a *Dharmic* tradition

Followers of *dharmic* traditions in the world estimated at **1,800,000,000+**

Followers of *Dharma* **23%** of world population

245 *Gurudwaras* in USA

First *Jain* temple in USA built in **1976**

121 languages spoken by 10,000 people or more in India

25 *Buddhist* Monastries in USA

First *Hindu* in America **1883**

Samskrit, Tamil are among the world's oldest languages, **5000+** years

40 Million+ *Hindu* manuscripts estimated across India

8 Main classical *Hindu* dance forms

300 Million Yoga practitioners worldwide

800+ *Hindu* Temples in USA

Jeffrey Armstrong | Kavindra Rishi
Founder VASA Vedic Academy of Sciences & Arts
Co-Chairman of VFA Vedic Friends Association

This wide ranging and informative text is a rich and enlightening doorway into the heart of the *Hindu Vedic Sanatan Dharma* culture of India. Its succinct and vivid descriptions illuminate the diverse and wide-ranging subjects of Indian culture, including all its many branches and profound subjects in a clear and approachable way. This beautiful and all-encompassing summary of the *Vedic* civilization should be in the library of anyone interested in global history and culture.

It is an artistic, profound, and elegant ambassador of the ancient treasures of the colorful and mysterious universal civilization that comes to life in its pages.

Darshana means to reveal and make visible, which is exactly what this beautiful book does.

Stephen Knapp | Sri Nandanandana dasa
Chairman of the Detroit *Krishna* Temple

Since time immemorial, *Vedic* culture, also known as *Sanatana-Dharma*, has provided humanity with a variety of tools to bring ourselves to the highest levels of self-development. This is in regard to all aspects of life, including developing one's health, or emotional, mental and intellectual capabilities, or even in one's career or occupational contributions, social harmony, and ultimately one's spiritual progress. This book, *"Darshana:* A Glimpse into the Hindu Civilization," gives insights into some of the ways by which a person can engage in such self-development, which are free to anyone. This book will also show the wide range of self-expression, such as dance, music, poetry, art, sculpture, and even architecture, that Hinduism has to offer on its spiritual path, along with many of the ancient advancements that came from this civilization over the centuries. The book is short, easy to read, and will expand the reader's view of what Hinduism and *Vedic* culture has to offer.

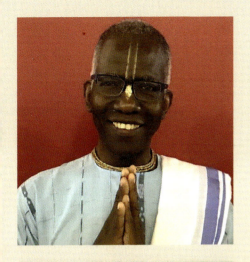

Balabhadra Bhattacarya dāsa
President, Vedic Friends Association

I am extremely proud of the work that HSS has done in preparing this truly inspiring coffee table book. It presents our *Dharmic* culture in a very dynamic and creative way. I am confident that it will be appreciated by a broad and diverse audience, and it will be my go to gift, especially for my many non-*Hindu* friends, and family members. *Hare Krishna.*

Suhag Shukla
Executive Director & Co-Founder, Hindu American Foundation

A colorful, concise yet comprehensive book about *Hindu* civilization. *Darshana*: A Glimpse into *Hindu* Civilization is a great resource for anyone wanting to learn or teach about *Hinduism*.
The explanations are easy to understand, and vivid imagery adds just the right touch to ensure readers will come away with the right understanding of *Hinduism* as a living, breathing tradition and the right impression of Hindus as a people.

Sadhvi Bhagawati Saraswati
President, Divine Shakti Foundation

I am so deeply impressed to see this beautiful publication "*Darshana*: A Glimpse into *Hindu* Civilization". It truly gives a sacred and exquisite glimpse into our rich, timeless tradition, heritage and culture which touch, teach and transform people from every walk of life. This book showcases, so magnificently, the history, the *dharma*, the theology, the art & architecture and the science as well as the daily implementable teachings of ayurveda, yoga and meditation which are of immeasurable value for all. I am sure that all who behold this gorgeous book will benefit greatly.